My Season Reflections

**Reflections and Illustrations
from Mom, Gma, Gigi and friend**
Sandra Brookens

MY SEASON REFLECTIONS

Published By: DNP Publishing

ISBN: 979-8-3302-8708-6

PRINTED IN THE UNITED STATES OF AMERICA

Foreword

By Nichol (Nikki P) Perricci

I am so excited to create this work for you. This is a book that my mom, Sandy, wrote for a few of her friends back home in Pennsylvania years ago.

Ever since I started helping people get their stories out there, I knew that one day, I would publish my mom's stories. As I sit and put this book together, I am overjoyed to share my mom with the world.

I know that you will enjoy her insight into the seasons, her drawings on each page, and the way she sees the world and shares it with us all. These reflections that Mom shares are from growing up in the country in a time free of technology and so much of the craziness of life that we all tend to stress over.

Those of us who have the pleasure of having her as an active part of our lives know her storytelling is a blessing. From stories told to me as a child, my children when they were young, and now her great-grandchildren, she can string a story like no one I know. Please enjoy this collection of "My Season Reflections" from Mom, Gma, Gigi and Friend… My mom, Sandy Brookens.

Introduction

Today, Feb 1, 2017 an idea came for a new book. Simple yet peaceful and fun. A new journey through memories of past, present, and future dreams. God created us with dreams, hopes, and imaginations.

Thank you to my daughter, Nikki, for helping me with her knowledge of computers. I love you! Also, to friends and family who have encouraged me to write and share. I thank my Heavenly

Father for blessing me and directing my path.

So, let's begin a journey together today. I pray this will bring back memories for you, cause you to dream again, and allow you to reflect on your past, present, and future.

Spring

I am the Rose of Sharon and
the Lily of the valley

Song of Solomon 2:1

The snow is Gone, and up through the

ground, I see green blades of grass.

Daffodils, crocus and lilies of the valley

poking up their colorful blossoms.

Have you ever smelled

Lily of the Valley?

So sweet and soft.

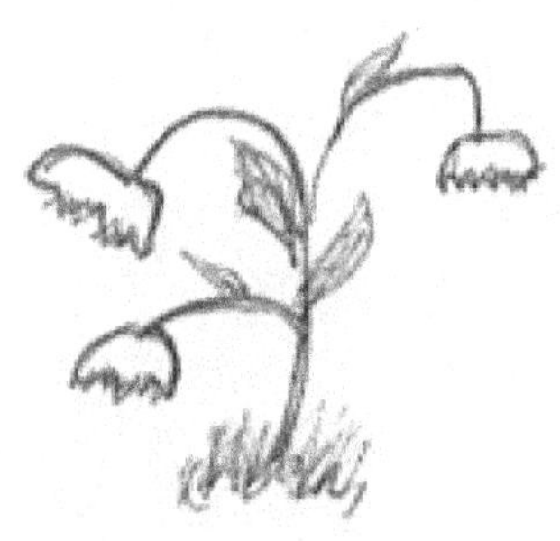

So then neither the one who plants nor the one who waters is anything, but God who causes the growth.

I Corinthians 3:7

Today, we tilled the garden, my father,

sister and I.

Planting will begin in 2 weeks.

Hope it's a good year for the garden.

And he shall be like a tree planted by the rivers of water that bringeth forth his fruit in his season; his leaf also shall not wither; and what so ever he doth shall prosper

Psalm 1:3

A day to run through the woods across
the creek from where we live in
Pennsylvania. Garden planted; grass
mowed.

Sun shining through the trees in rays of
beauty.

Today, we will make a new path
through the woods.

O taste and see that the Lord is good;

blessed is the man that trusteth in Him.

Psalm 34:8

Bare feet, shorts, and a cool shirt. Today is black raspberry picking day. My sister, Avis and I pick berries and eat them also.

'Ouch' careful of the thorns.

We won't even remember the heat or the thorns, as we taste the jelly our mother made for the family.

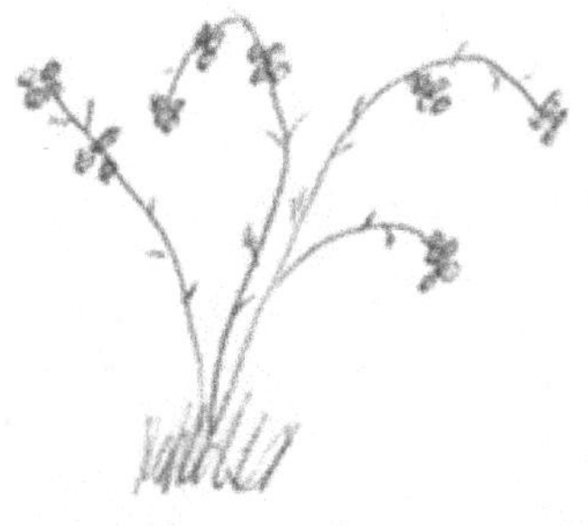

He covers the sky with clouds; he supplies the earth with rain and makes grass grow on the hills.

Psalms 147:8 NIV

As we watched from our neighbor's barn, a storm approached in the distance.

Have you ever laid on haybales and watched the rain, heard it hitting the tin roof, and smelled the rain and the hay?

If so, you are smiling at this memory.

MY SEASON REFLECTIONS

Summer

But who so ever drinketh of the water that I shall give him shall never thirst; but the water I shall give him shall be in him a well of water springing up into everlasting life.

John 4:14

The garden is growing so fast… as well

as the weeds!

Hot, tired but the weeding is done.

My, how a glass of cold water can

refresh the body!

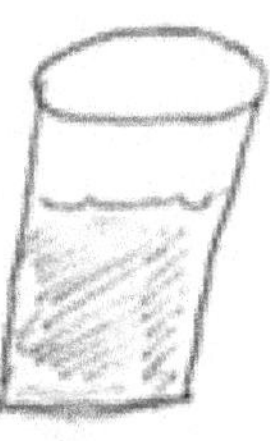

And God said, "Let the earth bring forth grass, the herb yielding seed and the fruit tree yielding fruit after his hand, whose seed is in itself, upon the earth." And it was so.

Genesis 1:11

Playday in our woods.

Exploring the fallen trees and eating wild sassafras roots and building a dam with stones across a branch of water in our creek.

We had a main creek, and it broke into two separate streams. We hear the call for 'dinner', already?!

Where did the day go?!

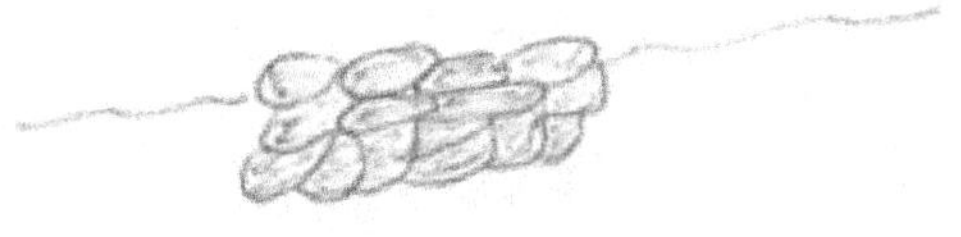

And he slept (Joseph) and dreamed the second time; and behold several ears of corn came up upon one stalk, rank and good.

Genesis 41:5

Started to pick the corn we planted in the spring. It's a new variety Dad wanted to try this year: Silver Queen.

When you live in the country, and you have corn for the meal… don't look for anything else… except butter, salt, and pepper.

Yummy, the Silver Queen is fit for a King.

The heavens declare the glory of God; and

the firmament show his handiwork.

Psalm 19:1

Happy 4th of July. We will be going to our local festival tonight. Music, food, rides, friends and neighbors. A perfect night as the fireworks start at 9:45pm.

Boom—boom—boom.

Beautiful bursts of colors; red, yellow, green, blue, purple glittering in the dark of night. Ooos and ahhs can be heard from the crowd.

And God created great whales, and every living creature that moveth, which the waters brought forth abundantly, after their kind and every winged fowl after his kind, and God saw that it was good.

Genesis 1:21

The hot weather makes us hurry our chores. The creek is waiting for us! Quick, change to a swimsuit and grab an innertube. We run into the woods.

We can hear the water as it goes downstream. Wahoo, no other way but to jump fully in at once. The cool water takes your breath for a minute.

As we float on our innertubes, on our tummies we can see small minnows and crayfish underneath us. Whoa… a trout just went under me!!

You will eat the fruit of your labor, blessings

and prosperity will be yours.

Psalms 128:12

Today, we picked the remaining crops
in the garden. Canning of fruit and
vegetables is almost done for the year.

Hard work, but we will enjoy eating the
fruits of our labors this winter.

Dad tilled the garden last evening.
Time for it to rest till next spring.

MY SEASON REFLECTIONS

For the Lord gives wisdom; From His mouth come knowledge and understanding.

Proverbs 18:15

It's a little chilly this morning.

Yesterday was Labor Day…

today, 1st day of school.

New clothes, shoes, and socks…

How I miss running barefoot in my

woods.

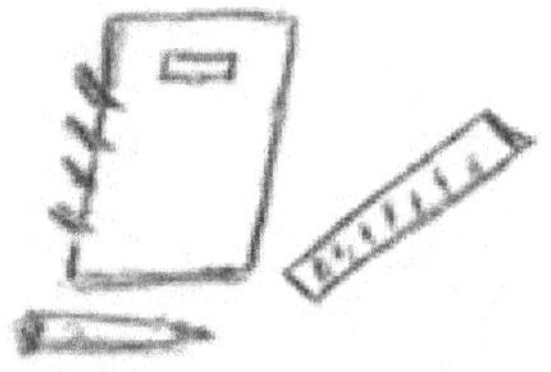

The grass withereth, the flower fadeth; but the word of our God shall stand forever.

Isaiah 40:8

The frost came quietly as I slept in my bed last night. The windows are frosted as we get ready for school.

Red, yellow, orange and brown leaves drop gentle to earth as nature has its way with the frost. Crunching underfoot on an Indian summer morning. We step outside and can see our breath in the air…

Remember breathing different ways to see the puffs of air change in shape. Made you smile again!

Keep me as the apple of the eye, hides me under the shadow of thy wings.

Psalms 17:8

The apple orchards are ready to be picked for the fall. My father works full time at the railroad making 'frogs.' In the fall, he helps a friend at his orchard.

It's cold and freezing in the fall mornings. He has a "Johnnie Warmer" in his pocket. A small metal warmer to warm his fingers, freezing quickly, picking the cold apples.

Oh yes, 'frogs' are the piece of rail track that when you pull a switch, and the train moves to a track beside it! Gotcha! You know real frogs come from tadpoles… Silly!

And after a time he (Samson) returned to take her and he turned aside to see the carcass of the lion, and behold, there was a swarm of bees and honey in the carcass of the lion.

Judges 14:8

I helped my father and his friend on the fall weekends. They sold the apples previously picked. Me! I have the job of filling jugs of cider made from the apples. Cold, sweet and delicious. One problem, the bees love it also. So, I try not to get stung as I fill the bottles.

People come from miles around for his apples and cider. Did you know, Jonathan apples when made into applesauce, turn the sauce a pink color? Leave skins on then strain. No artificial colors, God's design.

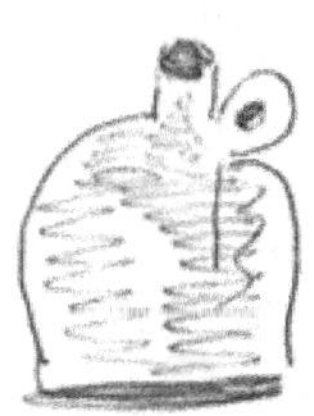

45

Winter

Enter his gates with thanksgiving and his courts with praise; give thanks to him and praise his name.

Psalms 100:4

Today we had another 8

inches of snow.

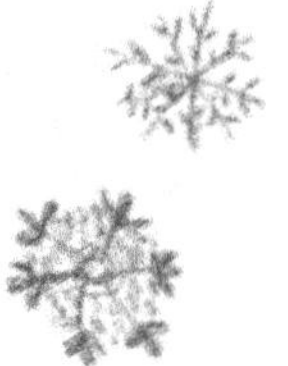

So far, we've had 12 inches.

Tomorrow is Thanksgiving. My mother

is a wonderful cook and baker. Turkey,

mashed potatoes, gravy, stuffing, fresh

frozen corn, candied sweet potatoes,

cranberry sauce, homemade pumpkin,

and apple pie with ice cream.

Do you remember smelling the turkey,

and your tummy was growling?

When do we eat??

For you shall go out in joy and be led forth in peace; the mountains and the hills before you shall break forth into singing, and all the trees of the field shall clap their hands.

Isaiah 55:12

Yeah, Christmas vacation.

2 weeks off and lots of fun. I asked for a certain doll this year and so did my sister.

My father always cuts a tree for our home.

It's always short and fat!!

Do you remember bubble lights and tinsel?

The more tinsel, the merrier.

His word became flesh and made his dwelling among us. We have seen his glory, the glory of the one and only Son, who came from the Father, full of grace and truth.

John 1:14

Christmas Eve has always been special to me. We go to my dad's home to visit our grandparents. Pappy Tolbert has a tree on a platform in the backroom.

Around the bottom is a small village with a train running thru it. It even blows a little puff of white smoke from its stack.

A couple of cookies and visiting cousins, aunts and uncles.

Saying where is he that is born King of the Jews? For we have seen his star in the east, and are come to worship him.

Matthew 2:2

Christmas Eve. It's 10:30pm, the air is cold as we bundle up. My sister and cousins choose to walk to church for candlelight service at 11:00pm.

As we step out into the night air, we see our breath as a cold air blows in our faces. Our boots crunch thru the snow on the road.

We laugh and talk about Christmas day and wondering what we may receive. The moon is full and the stars are shining brightly as we approach the church.

For unto you is born this day in the city of David a Saviour which is

Christ the Lord.

Luke 2:11

The church is ahead. Our manger scene is in the front: Mary, Joseph, and baby Jesus. We walk into the foyer, stomp off our boots and take off our coats. The door opens to the sanctuary.

Awe… the smell of pine and candles. The organ music in the air. A holy hush as the minister gives the message. "Jesus came for you and me". The lights dim, and individual candles are lit. We sing Silent Night together.

When we leave church, we are quiet on the way home.

Remembering 

the story

of Jesus.

Peace on Earth.

For by grace are ye saved through faith; and that not of yourselves; it is the gift of God; not of works lest any man should boast.

Ephesians 2:8

Christmas Day is finally here. I'm ready to open gifts at 5:00 am, but I know I have to wait till 7:00 am.

Rules from mom and dad… and NO peeking!

Even after becoming a grandparent, I'm still up at 5:00 am, but the family sleeps.

"No Peeking". I'll always be a kid at heart… Yes, I got the doll I wanted, and so did my sister.

For I know the plans I have for you, declares the Lord, plans to prosper you and not to harm you, plans to give you hope and a future.

Jeremiah 29:11 NIV

New Year's Day was one of football and relaxing.

The meal is always the same each year. Roasted Pork, sauerkraut, mashed potatoes, and peas.

It's a German custom over the years for prosperity for the new year!

But as it is written; Eye hath not seen, nor ear heard, neither have entered into the heart of man the things which God hath prepared for them that love him.

I Corinthians 2:9-10

January 1st, a new year begins… what will be the future?

Only our Heavenly Father knows our days as it should be.

We think we want to know the future, but… there is a growing process we need to go through between now and then to prepare us.

Just enjoy the day!

I will give thanks to you, Lord, with all my heart. I will tell of all your wonderful deeds.

Psalms 9:1

Valentine's Day… remember the decorated box and the excitement of preparing your little Valentine cards for your classmates?!

Everyone received a card, including the teacher. Classes done and late afternoon Valentines party.

Cupcakes and the passing out of the cards. Everyone waited until each person had all of his or her cards.

A fun and happy day. Whether a small valentine or a box of chocolate or a smile… it's a memory.

Life's short. Eat chocolate (dark).

May the God of hope fill you with all joy and peace as you trust in him, so that you may overflow with hope by the power of the Holy Spirit.

Romans 15:13

We are back to the beginning… Spring.

Not all our memories are happy, but we choose how we will live our life daily.

Step out, dream your dreams and make memories in the coming days. Life is short…

Remember the chocolate. Enjoy it and give someone a happy memory of you…

Let's continue to write our book of "seasons memories" for your family.

I've left pages for you to write some of
your memories.

Books are to be read, marked,

underlined, enjoyed and shared.

Continue your journey on the

following pages.

My Memory Pages…

Use these pages for your memories and yes, you can draw too ☺

My Memory Pages...

SANDRA BROOKENS

My Memory Pages…

69

MY SEASON REFLECTIONS

My Memory Pages...

SANDRA BROOKENS

My Memory Pages…

My Memory Pages…

72

SANDRA BROOKENS

My Memory Pages…

73

MY SEASON REFLECTIONS

My Memory Pages…

74

SANDRA BROOKENS

My Memory Pages…

75

My Memory Pages…

SANDRA BROOKENS

My Memory Pages…

77

My Memory Pages…

79